What Do Now?

A product manager's guide to strategy in the time of crisis

Randy Silver

CHRIS —
THANKS FOR
EVERYTHING,
ALWAYS!
— RANDY

SENSE &
RESPOND
PRESS

ISBN: 978-1-80068-401-0

Originally published in the United States by Sense & Respond Press, www.senseandrespondpress.com

Subsequently published by Out of Owls, outofowls.com

Out of Owls

CONTENTS

Acknowledgments

With love, thanks and gratitude to Anne & Rufus.

A good friend passed away from Covid-19 while this book was in production. This is dedicated to him, and to those who he left behind.

Wash your hands and call your friends.

Formatting note

This book was originally published in an electronic format only, with clickable links in the Resources at the end of each chapter.

As that doesn't (yet!) work in print, you can find all of these resources and links at:

outofowls.com/book

Vision, Purpose & Mission

This book is a product of - and a product for - the current crisis. A user story for it would read something like:

As a MEMBER OF A PRODUCT TEAM

I want to HAVE CONFIDENCE THAT I'M DOING THE MOST VALUABLE WORK THAT I CAN RIGHT NOW

So that I CAN HELP MY TEAM, MY COMPANY, MY FAMILY & FRIENDS, AND SOCIETY AT LARGE TO SURVIVE AND THRIVE

I started this book about a week into lockdown, when a single article spurred by conversations with friends and colleagues refused to stay short and simple. The things that kept coming up in conversations - about what to do, how to change our ways of working, and what we and our teams should be doing - were not simple questions, and focusing on them at the micro level missed the context of the kind of adjustments we actually need to make in our practice right now.

Two weeks later, it was done. Now it's in your hands.

This is not an exhaustive, meticulously-researched and anecdote-filled work of staggering genius which has been constructed to be useful forever. Rather, it's short, instructive, and meant to be useful right now. The intent is to help make sure you're asking the right questions about what you're doing and how you're doing it, to give some guidance on how to move forward, and to lead you to some great resources to further the work.

It's also short - you should be able to read this over lunch, or to dip in and out as needed.

If used correctly, it should spur good conversations within & across management and product teams - which is a not-insignificant part of the job on any day.

Stay safe, stay well, and wash your hands.

INTRODUCTION

There's a theory of evolutionary biology that seems especially pertinent at the moment called Punctuated Equilibrium. It's used to describe what we see happening in the fossil record: long periods that are relatively stable, followed by vast change over short periods. This is explained by a sudden, dramatic shift in the environment from an external stimulus, and it results in lots of species dying out - as well as the emergence of new ones, better suited to the new conditions.

It perfectly describes what we're observing now. Covid-19 has already had a massive effect on how we go about our daily lives. Our work and home-life routines have been thrown into chaos, to say nothing of what it was we're working on... for those of us lucky enough to even have work.

This is not a time to keep doing the same old thing. It's time to ensure that you, your team, your product and your firm are all positioned to survive and thrive in changing conditions.

So let's talk about strategy and roadmaps. (Yes, again.) But let's have a different chat this time.

A strategy is a statement of intent about an opportunity that your company has observed and what you plan to do to realise value from it. How you're going to do so is set out in a plan, which is often communicated in terms of a roadmap.

The roadmap might be good or bad; it might be theme- or timeline-based; it may have been created by you, collaboratively, or dictated by someone else. There are lots of great talks and resources out there about what makes a great roadmap and how best to develop and document your strategy. We won't go over that again here.

Whether you acknowledge it or not, your strategy - and therefore your roadmap - is made up of bets: if we do [this], it should have [impact]. Lining up a series of bitesize bets in a coherent way is how we create good, actionable strategies. Doing this well is rarer than we'd like, and a good superpower to have.

We also have to filter this through the constraints of what

capabilities - people, skills, technology, financing - are available to us to ground the plans in reality.

The next step for anyone using a product or design mindset is to try and validate the bets as quickly as possible, iterating to get to the best possible result under the constraints. Because if the bets don't work out, everything predicated on them is called into question.

Complicating this further is that these bets are in turn made up of two components: facts and assumptions. These are tricky beasts at the best of times - things that are assumed to be facts may turn out not to be validated. Assumptions can easily be misinterpreted as facts, especially when there's an emotional stake. Assumptions + emotions = opinions, which are whole lot harder to shift.

Another way of putting it: "It is difficult to get a man to understand something, when his salary depends on his not understanding it." (Upton Sinclair)

OK, last piece of this pyramid: the facts and assumptions themselves should be based on two things - the market landscape and your customer personas. Both of these things are, shall we say, a bit higgledy-piggledy at the moment. And if the base of the pyramid is wobbly, well...

This book is designed not to give you answers, but to make sure that you're asking the right questions. To be able to re-validate your current plan - and if needed, rebuild it under the current circumstances.

Followed step-by-step, the result will be a revised roadmap and release plan - something ready for the moment, validated by research, examination and conversation. The alternate approach, using the bits that resonate, to help resolve some of the tensions and uncertainties that you're experiencing is just as valid - the discussions that you'll have should be the outcomes you need to achieve the impacts within your teams.

It's based on 4 stages, diagrammed below. Some of the activities pop up multiple times, asking similar questions with new context.

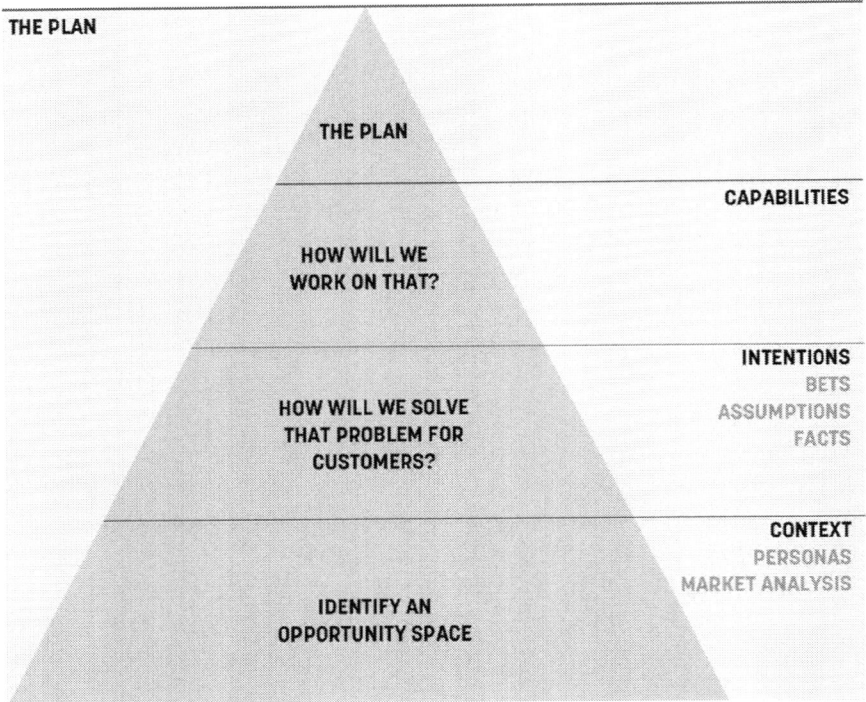

So: how do we get started?

PART 1: CONTEXT

In which we build the foundation of the pyramid, focusing on understanding our customers & the market; the problems and opportunities.

1
EXAMINE YOUR PERSONAS

"Habit is stronger than reason," George Santayana

We spend our working days trying to figure out what problems our customers have, their perceptions of them, how they're tackling the issue now, and ensuring that our solution is worth paying for. Baked into that are the habits that our customers have - and nothing is harder to change.

This is a moment, however, when habits are changing. People are consuming entertainment in new ways - conferences, concerts, social gatherings and events are moving online at a speed we haven't seen before. Baking is making a resurgence. Shopping habits are adjusting, as are local shops.

This is the perfect time to revisit your personas - pretty much everything in them is open for discussion again.

We use personas to map the problems people have, the situation they're in, and how they're likely to act. All of these things are subject to question right now, both in the short term and when the current crisis passes.

There are a number of questions we should be asking:

Who are we trying to help and what are their goals & obstacles?

And just as importantly - how does their perception of the goals and obstacles differ from ours? April Dunford goes deep into this in her book Obviously Awesome (she's also done a lot of great talks, available online, that give the basic idea), which primarily concerns itself on how to position your product.

What is their current situation? And how might that be different from their previous situation?

Are they using the product under the same conditions? Have their priorities changed?

Has their purchasing power been affected?

What relevant habits may be affected or changed by the crisis?

If you do change something for them right now, are they in a position to use it? As always, we need to marry what we want to do (what's good for the company) with what our customers believe they want. (This might be different from what they need, but that's a discussion for another day.)

Our ability to concentrate is, for many people, limited right now. This might be due to stress, crowded homes, unfamiliar working conditions, etc. While some habit changes might be accelerated right now, the cognitive load to get customers to adopt your change might be a barrier.

If you do change something for them right now, are they in a position to use it?

As always, we need to marry what we want to do (what's good for the company) with what our customers believe they want. (This might be different from what they need, but that's a discussion for another day.)

There's an added complication now: the ability to distribute and implement new products or services is highly impaired. This might be due to lockdown, supply chain, manufacturing - or, for B2B, even the ability to deal with corporate procurement and security practices.

Any decisions that you make right now without asking these questions have a high likelihood of being wrong.

If you find that you can't answer them, it's time to go back to basics and spend a week or two on basic discovery/research activities to find out. As per Teresa Torres, we should be doing continuous discovery anyway - these activities shouldn't be something we dust off only in times of crisis.

This is a unique situation, however - and in the spirit of never wasting a good crisis, think about how you can do this better. Can you enlist sales and marketing people to help with the activities? Spend more time listening into or reading support requests? Where can you get real, actionable information from current and potential customers, how can you best review and synthesise it, and how can you use that to build a shared understanding both inside and outside of your product teams?

Resources:
·   User Persona templates
·   How do you do remote research with customers and potential customers? The Insider Insight technique is especially relevant right now, focusing on using conversations between people who already have a relationship to get you insight into their habits, feelings and perceived problems. It's perfectly suited to remote situations.
·   UK Government's guide to Conducting Remote user research during the Corona crisis - https://www.gov.uk/service-manual/user-research/conducting-user-research-while-people-must-stay-at-home-because-of-coronavirus
·   Teresa Torres writes a lot about continuous discovery at ProductTalk

2
Revalidate the market landscape

Before your product was launched, someone (hopefully!) did some work mapping out the competitive landscape - everything from who the dominant players are, where and how they operate, their pricing, their branding and positioning, and where the significant opportunities lie.

This work should also be updated at least once a year, or anytime something significant happens in your space. That could be a merger or acquisition, the launch of a new capability by a competitor, someone else entering your competitive space, or - as contracts refer to it - an act of God.

In the context of contractual law, God has well and truly acted now.

There is no precedent in living memory for the situation we find ourselves in. The decisions we made before the pandemic hit are up for review - but so are the decisions our competitors made. And unless you have some divine help or engage in illicit practices to figure out what decisions they're making now, it's going to be nigh impossible to predict how they're going to operate in the near future.

When you start factoring in the unknowns about financial markets, elections, supply chains, new or suspended/amended regulations, and even how changes in corporate leadership will affect your competitors, vendors and suppliers, partners and resellers, etc... this quickly becomes an impossible task.

So why is it still worth doing?

Because it's always an impossible task. Any forward-looking analysis committed to paper is wrong from the moment it's published. That's hardly the point, and ignores nearly all of the value.

The artefact that you produce is not what helps you. The conversations that your management team had to reach these conclusions, the documentation of risks and assumptions, the visual mapping and shared view - these are invaluable.

This is the type of conversation that any good

organisation should be having on a regular basis. Using this period to ensure that you're actually doing it, and to create the kinds of habits that will help you to survive and thrive - that's invaluable.

There's no one right way to guarantee that you'll get the intended outcome, though there are a number of avoidable mistakes. These boil down to not having the conversation at all, or to having them in ways that are not genuine. We've all walked out of meetings where people didn't come to a shared understanding, that they simply talk past one another.

There are a couple of methodologies that work well to organise people for these conversations.

Strategy consultants make use of Scenario Planning (sometimes Scenario & Contingency Planning) as a methodology to guide these conversations. The basic idea is to create a set of plausible ways that events could turn out - for example, a Covid-19 vaccine becoming available in 3 months, 6 months, 12 months, 18 and 24 months. Under each of those cases, what's different about the market? Your customers? Your cash flow?

What would you need to do to thrive under each of these circumstances? What are the key early indicators that your plans are working or not going as intended?

Scenario planning isn't something most Product people use regularly, but many of them have experience with mapping. (Service Designers also make extensive use of this approach, and it's a super power right now. Nothing sets the stage better for constructive disagreement or alignment than an easy-to-understand artefact.)

Maps are pervasive in the product world. There's any number of flavours - roadmaps, journey maps, experience maps, service maps, emotion maps, user story maps, etc.. (Ever seen Best in Show? It's like Harlan Pepper reciting varieties of nuts.) We'll go into more detail on these in Chapter 4.

There's one approach that's specifically appropriate at this stage, Simon Wardley's particular implementation of Value-Chain Mapping. It comes with a bit of a steep learning curve, but can be invaluable for gaining a better understanding of where the opportunity lies in a market.

The key difference in his approach is both semantic and philosophical - he makes a distinction between maps and diagrams that matters at this stage:

A map must be visual and context specific. It must have components but more than this it requires an anchor, position and movement. The quickest way I know to determine if something is a map or not is to move a component (i.e. use movement) and see if this changes the meaning of what is being looked at. - Simon Wardley

Very simply: the relative positions of two things on a map matter. When we're trying to build a shared context, it's very easy to talk past each other - and it's even easier to do so when we're not next to each other, reading all of the non-verbal cues that tell you how other people are reacting.

While diagrams are great for providing context and introducing ideas, there's significant benefit from the use of a formal map-based approach at this stage.

Resources:

- An introduction to Wardley Mapping: Bits or pieces?: Is my diagram a map?
- Scenario Planning and Strategic Forecasting
- Susana Lopes did a nice overview of how Product Managers at Onfido handle market analysis in her Mind the Product article, Tools to Help Product Managers Think Strategically and Commercially
- Could you have predicted the current circumstances - and how can you prepare for the next major change in your field? Rita McGrath talks about how to recognise what she calls Time Zero events in her book *Seeing Around Corners*, and breaks down the technique in her blog post, Everything Old Is New Again: Why Fast Fashion Is Facing an Inflection Point.
- *The Invincible Company*, from Alex Osterwalder's Strategyzer, also deals with how to prepare for and handle change.
- In their book *Agile Conversations*, Jeffrey Fredrick and Douglas Squirrel document five specific conversations that

should be happening in healthy organisations (Trust, Fear, Why, Commitment and Accountability) and how to ensure that you're getting value from each.

PART 2: INTENTIONS

In which we move to the next level, focussing on how we intend to create solutions.

3
QUESTION YOUR PRIORITIES

At this stage, we've learned something - most likely, that at least some of the conclusions from any pre-lockdown discovery activities are no longer valid. If the foundation we built our planning on is no longer solid, then we need to examine if the problems we aimed to solve and the market opportunity are still correct.

That calls into question any planning we'd previously committed to, including any
goals, roadmaps or release plans that might be floating around.

If that's the case, should we be working towards the same goals? It's time to ask if we're still on the right track.

There are two essential questions to ask:

1.   Is there something we can do that helps with the current situation?

2.   Is what we're currently working on still the best thing to do?

Let's take those in turn:

Is there something we can do that helps with the current situation?

If so, scrap/pause your roadmap and do that.

There are caveats - you still need to figure out how to keep the lights on. To do right by your team and employees, as well as for everyone else.

There are plenty of ways to help - providing PPE and ventilators, supporting essential services, helping the vulnerable, entertaining and educating children, promoting mental and physical wellbeing, ensuring the wellbeing of your business, etc.

But there's one big way to be wrong in this situation, and that's by failing to ask the question at all.

Is what we're currently working on still the best thing to do?

We've learned a lot by taking a hard look at our personas and the market landscape. That doesn't mean we have the correct answers at this stage - but we should be able to recognise when something is no longer valid.

This is where agile organisations come into their own. You should have the ability to have a good conversation about the possibilities, as well as the experience to conceive of some experiments which can be run quickly to find out if shifting your priorities is worthwhile. Does your firm have the capability to do something that will make a short-term difference - or are you trying to build an experimental rescue sub just because it sounds cool?

It's no good having this conversation at the individual team level. This is a leadership question first - one that must be made in terms of both the short-term and long-term financial outlook - and then spread out wide to the rest of the organisation. As always, management can set the direction of intent, but it's the people and teams closest to the problem that can best identify how it can be done, what problems might arise, and what they actually need to succeed.

Remember: having the right answer is important, but first you need to be sure to be asking the right question.

Resources:

·   Giff Constable's advice:
https://twitter.com/giffco/status/1246195155218161669?s=20

4
Map your facts and assumptions

Now we have the basics to proceed:
- An idea of what the situation is for our customers, what their problems are, and what they perceive their problems to be;
- A set of plausible scenarios about the market landscape and how it might unfold; and
- An idea of what direction we want to move in.

But we're also not working in normal circumstances. We'll get to how to do the work in the next section, but there's one last thing we need to acknowledge: more so than ever, we're operating in unknown territory.

We're working quickly, with blind spots that we're not always going to be aware of, in a constantly changing situation.

We already covered the dangers that the information we based our decisions on - both facts and assumptions - might not be as safe as we believe. It's time to revisit the Scenario Planning process covered in Chapter 2, from a new angle. This time, we're going to re-examine the story we've told ourselves to get to this point and validate the strategy.

Paul Saffo's mantra of "Strong opinions, weakly held" is the ideal we strive towards here - but even the best of us, as individuals or teams, are going to be tested on how well we adhere to it. And wherever we have a potential problem on getting people to agree on a shared understanding, there are frameworks and exercises which can be employed to move forward.

None of these are perfect. None of them are correct. But the right one for your situation - the one that you feel comfortable explaining, and which your audience is ready to embrace - has the capability to cut through the morass and avoid what Stephen Colbert once referred to as a "truthiness," (the idea that something that feels right is more important than actually being right).

A few ways of doing this:

1. Assumptions mapping

David Bland's talk on this technique comes with a handy template that marries feasibility, viability and desirability with a 2x2 matrix to generate an action plan. The basic idea is to start by understanding what your stakeholders or team wants to learn - and then digging into all of the assumptions that form the basis for your current approach and attitude.

2. Impact mapping

Another way of approaching this is to start from the Impact that you want to see - not what features you release or products you have in the market, but what difference they'll have. Tim Herbig has a great introduction to this, detailing the differences between outputs, outcomes and impacts - and how to use them to orient your strategy.

3. Theory of Change

Commonly used in the field of international aid, Theory of Change is another approach that starts with the desired outcome, the current conditions - and then helps fill in the messy middle.

4. Dragon mapping

This is my own variation on these techniques, loosely based on a talk I've done about Discovery practices, the Riskiest Assumption Test, and South Park's infamous episode in which gnomes have a business plan that has three simple steps:

Phase 1: Collect Underpants
Phase 2: ?
Phase 3: Profit

It's a fairly simple method, and can be applied to whatever artefacts your company is already using, from a business plan to a journey map. At every step, ask one question of your team and stakeholders: "For this to happen, what has to be true?"

Document all the answers, and then clearly map them as facts (things that are objectively, verifiably true) and assumptions (everything else).

The next step is to rank the assumptions based on risk: if this was not true, what would the impact be?

You now have a prioritised list of things to run experiments on - and, when done well, the support of stakeholders to do so. There may be times when there isn't the appetite to do validation - and if things are going well, there may not be the need. But the first time something underperforms, you now have the framework for a productive conversation on how to figure out what went wrong, as well as how to move forward.

There's one more thing that needs to be done at this stage - and it's something that we're liable to miss when adjusting our strategy at pace. Decisions made quickly need to be examined rigorously. Firms that have a culture of learning fast (sometimes referred to as failing fast) are optimised for this, but it's something we need to be especially conscious of now.

We need to ask what could go wrong - how could the decisions we are making now potentially harm our customers, the wider public, or our company's reputation. Best intentions are no excuse when things are done badly and create harm.

Roisi Proven's Black Mirror test is a great exercise to elucidate the unintended consequences of your decisions. Simply ask: if your product/service/feature was going to be the subject of an episode of Black Mirror, what would the plot be?

(If you haven't watched the show, substitute in The Twilight Zone, or the central part of a Charles Stross or Cory Doctorow novel - the central issue here is that we almost always talk only to a limited group of people when considering or making decisions. Ensuring that your team has a diversity of background and viewpoints can mitigate against this, but the exercise is valuable in any case.)

The answers to this then form a risk register for you to mitigate and plan against, and inform the implementation decisions you make.

<u>Resources</u>:

- Nandini Jammi, the co-founder of the Sleeping Giants campaign, has a number of great talks with advice about brand safety. (https://nandinijammi.com/speaking/)
- Dragon Mapping: outofowls.com/dragonmapping
- Strong Opinions weakly held
- South Park, ???? PROFIT!!!!
- What's the Worst That Could Happen? By Roisi Proven

PART 3: CAPABILITIES

In which we review the feasibility of our intentions.

5
REVIEW YOUR CAPABILITIES

At the best of times, we struggle to deal with the connection between quality and quantity. When it comes to understanding how long something is going to take we run into all sorts of issues.

The Mythical Man-Month. The idea that throwing more people at something makes it go faster. The most common retort to this is that 9 pregnant women can't have a baby in 1 month, but my favourite is Randall (@rkoutnik) Koutnik's tweet: 'I bought my boss two copies of *The Mythical Man Month* so he could read it twice as fast'

Estimating complexity isn't straightforward. Liz Keogh's take on confidence in estimation is a brilliant illustration on the risks we too often ignore.
1.   Just about everyone in the world has done this.
2.   Lots of people have done this, including someone on our team.
3.   Someone in our company has done this, or we have access to expertise.
4.   Someone in the world did this, but not in our organisation (and probably at a competitor).
5.   Nobody in the world has ever done this before.

Quality doesn't have a linear relationship with effort, resource or even experience - though all of them do help.
Under normal circumstances, we're bad at this - prediction of future events with any level of complexity involved is something humans fool ourselves into thinking we're good at. Our biases creep in quickly, and we have no relevant prior evidence to base the current scenario on - how can we possibly be accurate about what will come next?
What we need to do is reduce the variables. We've already done that - to the extent that it's possible - in terms of our customers and the market. Now we need to take a hard look at ourselves.

The tools that we normally use have been refined and optimised under normal trading conditions. Whatever you use - whether it's gut feel, estimates, story points and burndown charts, work in progress - are going to lie to you unless you refactor the underlying assumptions.

Who is available? And how available are they?

It's likely that your team is not at full strength right now. People may not be available due to furlough, being ill or caring for someone else. Or - a better scenario - they may have their attention divided by having to also look after children, with school and childcare not available.

They're also dealing with stress and anxiety. It's been said many times, by many people, but this scenario is not working from home. It's not working remotely. It's working under crisis conditions.

It's not the new normal, and it should never become so.

Don't expect everyone to simply adjust and get back to normal productivity.

When my son was born, my brother gave me some advice: think in terms of 2-week timeframes. No one's sleeping and things are tough? This phase will pass and things will get better. Everything's calm and going well? This too shall pass, expect things to become turbulent again.

Everyone's going through this now, and we're not all on the same schedule. Expect things to remain changeable for quite some time.

The other scenario I see too often is where entire teams or departments have been either furloughed or fired, but the expectations have not been changed. Please don't be the person who does this - it's not a sustainable situation when the remaining staff members are in their ideal situation, and it's doubly damaging now.

What constraints is your team working under?

Even when people are available, they're working under different conditions. They might not have access to a comfortable desk and chair, to a speedy internet connection, to a quiet space, to physical artefacts that are in the office, or to resources on the corporate network.

People might need to start using new tools and get used to new ways of working. Training and mastery can be a challenge

Activities and processes that were regular and predictable might not be so today.

What tools do you normally use? Which are not currently available? Or are not suited to remote usage?

One of the great benefits of co-locating is the ability to use the physical environment to orient your teams and create ambient awareness both of the work that you're doing and the context it sits in. We put up posters, announcements, awards, maps, dashboards and alerts - things that you may not even consciously be aware of half the time.

We can do these things using remote tools - but it's difficult to zoom in and out to different levels on a laptop screen. We use our environment in so many ways that it's only when it's not available that we start to appreciate it.

At larger firms, it's common for certain tools to only be available on the corporate network, and the rapid proliferation of this pandemic means that many people may not have either a corporate device or VPN access. (HR and Finance systems seem to be especially vulnerable to this.)

What's your release cycle?

If you release iterations daily or weekly, there's a good chance you have the communication, marketing and technical infrastructure to handle a change to your plan so that you can respond to the current situation in near-real time.

If you release quarterly or less frequently, strongly consider whether you're prepared to handle a quick update - as well as whether your customers would welcome it.

Do you know how to set up and run experiments? And how to analyse them?

As the philosopher Ferris Bueller said, "Life moves pretty fast. If you don't stop and look around once in a while, you could miss it."

We can be so busy reacting to things that we lose the context of why we initiated a piece of work. It's important to remember - how can we forget? - how fast everything is changing at the moment, so anything that we do in the moment has to be treated as an experiment.

That means that we also need to have the right setup to rigorously review what we did, what we expected to happen, and what actually did happen.

Yes, this is how we should work anyway - but how many of us actually practise it all of the time? This isn't the time to skip this step... and it may actually be an opportunity to bring others along on the journey so that this practice becomes embedded in your company's regular ways of working.

'May actually be' is doing an awful lot of work in the previous paragraph. Being honest with yourself is important - if you don't have the expertise or access to it, this may be the worst possible time to introduce experimentation into your practice. Another contra-indicator would be if you don't have the right environment to bring in the type of information these processes generate.

Remember, a really successful experiment will tell you what's not working. Is that something your team, peers and stakeholders are ready to hear right now, or will it only cause confusion?

Experimentation should help make things clearer for your organisation. If introducing it now won't do that, it's not serving any useful purpose.

What can you do better - and not do as well - now?

We perceive that there are some things we can only do in the office or when sitting with a customer. Here's what I've been hearing from product people:

Things that are easier:

• Create roadmaps and write strategy documents/requirements
• Any high level planning, including getting clear focus and guidance from time-poor experts
• Standups
• Stakeholder meetings have been more efficient.

- For some, being able to carve out time to focus without interruption
- I'm finding the situation is forcing people to be more intentional in their communication
- Finding time to do administrative deep work, manage my inbox, and research current tech trends has been much easier during the lockdown.
- Holding creative workshops and prioritisation sessions using tools like Miro - attendees seem more focused

Things that are harder:
- Managing development
- Design sprints
- Breaking down the barriers for people who don't already use collaborative tools
- Staying in touch with the team
- Co-ordinating small ad-hoc requests
- Reintroducing comfort to those that relied subtle signals from the office-based teams,
- We ran a few user research sessions remotely, which was really difficult both operationally and also to find insights that are meaningful/credible.
- User research is a bit more challenging but UserZoom has been a good resource.
- Team retrospectives

Things that feel impossible:
- Customer interviews
- Remote user testing when the demographics focus on users who aren't tech-savvy and where internet speed is very not reliable
- Large-scale discovery work (need physical space and lots of whiteboards!),
- Getting everyone to talk on a large social call
- With the extra burden on telecom bandwidth, virtual face-to-face interactions have been next-to-impossible.

There's a nice range here, with some people finding opportunities and others challenges from the same situations. One friend found it useful that more senior stakeholders were showing up at meetings, as it increased decision velocity - while others found that the new attention was unwelcome and caused disruption in meetings that used to run smoothly.

Surprisingly, even some of the most intensive activities can be adapted successfully. There's an entire cottage industry around Design Sprints, and more than one party has already pivoted to running - and teaching others - how to do them remotely.

Most of us just haven't developed the practices to do our normal activities this way because we haven't had to.

We can even engineer serendipity in remote communities - tools like Shuffl and Donut can be used in Slack to pair up random people for chats, to great effect.

There are a lot of great conversations taking place about how to handle these things - out of necessity, there's been a lot of interest and development in this area. Stay engaged and you'll be able to find more good tips and guidance than you can possibly digest - pick something that sounds good and give it a try.

What can you do better remotely?

Strangely, there are some things that we can do even better remotely than in the office. You've probably taken the odd day to work from home - or from a quiet corner of the office - to get some documentation done. Or research, training, filing expenses, data crunching, etc. Depending on your current set-up, working remotely might not provide the kind of setup to optimise for these activities.

One thing we can take advantage of is that our customers are in the same situation. While we often ask product teams about the last time they talked to a customer, the question that should be asked is the last time that they actually listened to one.

That happens far more rarely than it should. Rarer yet is actually learning from our customers - and using that learning to adjust how we tackle their problems.

Remote discovery, when done well, can allow us to do just that. Whether it's using diary studies, getting people to document their conditions with photos or a video tour, or getting in touch with people on a video call, the tools to do so are widely available. Twenty years ago - before the availability of home broadband, mobile phones, laptops and tablets, - it would have been impossible to do the kind of timely remote research that we can achieve today.

What can your team accomplish under these conditions ?

Teams get a reputation for what they can accomplish in a fixed time-frame, and expectations for that are hard to shift. We're not wired to change our estimates very easily, and that can lead to real problems when the perception doesn't match up to the delivery.

John Cutler's explanation of why it's important to limit Work in Progress is always relevant, but especially so when it's hard for people to visualise a team's productivity. It's critical that we spend time on this now - first re-evaluating what we can expect from ourselves, then applying it to how we set expectations and limits with our peers, partners, and stakeholders.

Resources:
- The Ultimate Guide to Remote Designs Sprint by AJ&Smart
- Liberating Structures - Introduction
- The In the Ether meetups have an open-source format for virtual, lean coffee meetups that is easily adaptable for meetings. (I run the Product in the {A}ether offshoot.)
- Customer Discovery In the Time Of the Covid-19 Virus

6
REVIEW YOUR WAYS OF WORKING

It's a cliche to compare our diaries to an advanced Tetris level - but this has long been a problem for most people I know. It's gotten even worse during the lockdown - between everyone's sudden availability (no travelling) and competing priorities (parenting, etc), many of the people I talk to are stuck on calls all day long.

This is an anti-pattern at the best of times, and we have a unique opportunity to make some changes. Companies and teams that succeed at working remotely share some common patterns:

They meet when they need to - and use asynchronous communication for everything else

Stand-ups are an amazing way to build cohesion across a team, tackle emerging problems quickly, and reinforce priorities on a daily basis. They can also turn into pro forma status updates, and people who work across multiple teams can lose their entire morning stand-up hopping.

A lot of the daily and weekly ceremonies we have were established in diaries sometime in the mists of time, and never leave. It's time to go Marie Kondo on your diary: Does this meeting spark joy - or at least provide value? If not, try replacing it with something else.

If you get value out of a meeting but the rest of the team doesn't, seek to understand why - can the meeting be shorter? Held less often? Can you get the same value from another approach?

They've evolved to use common tools and structures.

While we want to encourage everyone to be as autonomous as possible, it can be a massive challenge when everyone stores their key documents and artefacts in a different place and format. There's a complexity tax to pay in terms of providing good communication and collaboration across teams, but it's also our job to make sure that the tax is minimal.

Find something that works in a way that is good enough to provide context and information, but which doesn't dominate your day - something which allows you to work well with others, but still gives you the time to actually do your job.

Too often, even the best tools designed for organising our information fail. They rely on rigorous usage of naming conventions, folder structures, user permissions, or being able to divine how someone else thought it should be named. Even the tools that do intelligent search fail because of the sheer volume of cruft we save.

There's a reason Sharepoint used to be referred to as a document coffin - where information goes to die. No tool will ever solve the problem of poor common practices.

They have clear channels for effective communication.

Slack, Teams, Twist, WhatsApp, Facebook Workplace... whatever tools your team has for messaging, there's a real challenge around getting the right information to the right people at the right time, at the appropriate level of prioritisation.

We all use lots of different communication methods instinctively, and there's no one-size-fits-all approach. Anyone who's ever done any kind of project management has learned the basic lesson that some people respond to email, some to phone calls, some to instant messages... and some you have to walk over and sit next to them before they'll respond.

We see the same things in our home lives, and we adjust natively. We know which friends we can text with, which live on Instagram or Facebook, which are going to answer if we actually ring them on the phone. We know that our grandparents will rarely be using the same channels as our kids - so we use the methods that work for each. And we kludge it together when we need to get them all together.

But teams that work well together have figured out some basic rules. They may talk 1:1 using whatever's at hand, but team communications and documents have a single, agreed pattern.

They've figured out the difference between social

communication and priority communication. They'll have channels for regular chat, but these often get overwhelmed after a while - so they'll have a separate channel for urgent or priority messages. People quickly learn when to use each channel, the group works to enforce the norms, and the norms change as the team's requirements evolve.

They don't micro-manage.

This is a bad time for micro-managers and people who equate presenteeism with productivity. Being at your desk can't be confused with getting the work done, except in the rare circumstance where being visibly available is the success criteria.

Managers and organisations who have already learned the lessons to prioritise outcomes over outputs are set up to thrive right now. Getting to the outcomes in trying circumstances may be a challenge - but it's going to have a higher correlation with success than pure busywork.

Doing this well is a superpower. It means that the desired impacts and how each team's work ladders up to the overall visions must be clearly articulated, disseminated and understood.

Setting clear objectives and letting teams have the autonomy to deal with it - within confined conditions - is key to success in these conditions.

Given all that, here are a few things we can do to level-up how we work in confinement conditions - and what we can do that'll make us even more effective when this situation ends:

1. Hold retrospectives with your team, your peers and your stakeholders. Figure out what's working and not working in terms of communication and process.

2. Retire or change practice for any meetings, reports or documentation that is not doing the job that it needs to do. That can be changing the frequency or duration, the format, or eliminating it entirely.

3. Manage for serendipity. When we're not co-located, we don't have the hallway/water-cooler/kitchen conversations. We don't have team lunches or drinks. You'll need to intentionally create these - whether it's random

pairings for virtual coffees, team games/social activities, etc.

4.   Change your meeting formats. Use icebreakers to make sure everyone is involved early on - and that their microphone and camera is on. Make sure you engage everyone regularly - seek feedback. As we don't have the ability to make eye contact, try using hand signals to indicate support, or when you have something to add. A good way of encouraging people to participate in meetings is to make sure that they say something early.

PART 4: THE PLAN

In which we get back to focusing on execution.

7
FOCUS AND EXECUTE

As always, this is the easy part. We've done all the preparation, built the right structures and set up everyone for success. We have the underpants, we've put in the thought as to what Step 2 is, so now: profit!

Not so fast. Success is a combination of preparation and luck. Not having either is a guarantee of failure, but having only one is not sufficient for success.

While we can't manufacture luck reliably, there are some things we can do to encourage it - and to ensure that we're ready when it comes our way.

Explain it to me like I'm a 6-year old: Make sure you can explain how any changes affect both the work you're doing today and the longer term strategy.

Product managers need to be able to work both tactically and strategically, to keep the small details and the big picture in their head at any one time - and to understand how the two relate. That means any changes at either end have to be considered all the way through to the other end. This is hard at the best of times, and many product people struggle with explaining it clearly to everyone else.

Ha Phan recently tweeted:

System thinking; seeing how the smallest bet scales into the biggest bet. One of my engineers asked me when the bigger vision [came] to me, and my answer was that I'd always seen it... I've received "the look" many times after I try to explain. A previous PM I used to work with used to tell me that I have to let people catch up to me.

John Cutler detailed an exercise he runs with teams to provide context over multiple timescales for his newsletter, *The Beautiful Mess*. Most of our planning is readily understandable at the daily/weekly/sprint levels, there's usually some quarterly goals and an annual plan, he explains - but when's the last time you tried to connect your afternoon's activities to understand how it impacts the annual plan? Or the longer term strategy?

As he explains,

In doing this exercise with many teams, I've come to see how often teams bump into a "messy middle" problem. Work in the near term is clear (people come into work and want something to do). Work in the long-term fits on a slide in an executive's deck. Turns out making slides is easy.

It is the messy middle bets/missions in the 1-3 month and 1-3 quarter range that are far less coherent.

The takeaway: You need to be able to understand the impact of any decisions you make now, at both the micro and macro ends of the scale - but so does everyone else. We can't afford to have people working in a volatile environment without a clear sense of how their work contributes to and impacts the strategy.

Getting the context clear is job #1 - but it doesn't need to be a solo activity. Get other people involved.

Make sure everyone's on the same page.

We've already touched on the importance of communication, but there's one more technique for alignment that is both easy to implement and incredibly useful. The concept of Briefing and Back-Briefing is an old Prussian military technique which ensures that management doesn't simply dictate what they expect to happen.

Instead, the initial strategy briefing is followed up by the individual teams preparing a back-briefing that describes what they understand their objective to be and how they plan to achieve it.

As these individual plans - created by the teams who will actually do the work, who are the closest to the problem and know their capabilities - are collated, any gaps, misunderstandings, or unintended consequences become clear.

Roadmaps are a useful way to broadcast the Briefing side of this - but the essential work of revisiting and reviewing these artefacts, as well as pairing them with detailed release plans , is the part that's too often left out. These activities can constitute the Back-Briefing.

Remember the basic principle of Agile - er, agile

There's a furious debate in the more obsessed parts of the Product community about what the term 'agile' actually means today, focusing on the difference between the basic principles ('agile') and the strict framework-based approach that is sometimes sold by consultancies ('Agile').

For the purpose of this essay, I'm going to make it simple: Agile teams and organisations are able to assimilate new information and change both what their goal is and how they plan to achieve it. They review this regularly, and change - or iterate - their approach using whatever evidence is at hand to best inform their efforts.

That means that, quite simply, agile teams and organisations have learned the lesson that the great philosopher Mike Tyson imparted when he said, "Everybody has a plan until they get punched in the mouth."

Either you lay down or you get back up, adjust, and try another approach.

What that means for us is that the implementation of our strategy is not going to result in a straight line, or even a neat curve. It will have fits and starts. It will go up and down, double back on itself, and - if we're lucky and prepared - trend in the right direction. The best explanation of this I've come across was Ted Danson's overview of the Jeremy Bearimy timeline in *The Good Place*. (If you haven't watched it yet, spoiler alert. Also, what are you waiting for?)

Separate your operational and strategic timelines

There's a big difference between what your business is already doing and what you're planning to do next. Don't fail your customers who are counting on you to remain operationally sound while you work on the next thing.

It may be that to achieve that reliability, your efforts need to be applied to shoring up your operational efforts. Or to plugging gaps that have been created by lack of availability of people, resources or tools. That comes first.

Be both intentional and realistic about what changes need to be made to your strategy, why these are needed, and when they can be realised.

Don't stop learning - and take the time to reflect

We've already covered the idea of Strong Opinions, Weakly Held, but it's worth revisiting. As circumstances change and new information becomes available, make sure that you're challenging yourself on a regular basis. To do that, you'll need to build time into your schedule to allow for it.

In his appearance on *The Product Experience* podcast, John Cutler told my co-host Lily Smith and I:

"All product managers should set aside [time] every day to do the deeper work... product managers are so reactive, they're always struggling to keep up – yet if you don't do the deeper work... you're always going to be on the back foot. Not doing the busy work – but actually revisiting assumptions."

Resources:
- Briefing & Back-Briefing was documented by Stephen Bungay in his book *The Art of Action*; I first discovered it on the invaluable *Troubleshooting Agile* podcast; and Ask Agger published a good article on how to put the technique into action in a workshop.
- John Cutler, *The Beautiful Mess* 14/53: 1s and 3s
- Roadmaps are Dead! Long Live Roadmaps! by C. Todd Lombardo
- The 666 roadmap | Inside Intercom
- In his talk at MTP Engage Hamburg 2018 (Owning Agile), Jeff Patton gave an overview of techniques of how to keep your team - and the wider organisation - focused on the outcomes and impacts of any current work.

AFTERWORD

This book was written in the midst of the Covid-19 lockdown from central London, based on observations and conversations I've had with members of the product community across the US, UK, Europe and Asia.

It's meant to be part of an ongoing conversation about what we're learning and how we're adapting. All proceeds from this edition will be going to support Covid-19 relief efforts. If you've gotten a copy without paying for it, please make a donation of your own.

Let me know how you've used this guide and what's been working for you.

ABOUT THE AUTHOR

Randy Silver is a product consultant and coach who has been working in product roles across the US and UK for 20 years.

A recovering music journalist and editor, he launched Amazon's music stores in the US and UK; he's also worked across sectors including museums and arts groups, online education, media and entertainment, retail, and financial services.

Randy held Head of Product roles at HSBC and Sainsbury's, where he also directed their 100+-person product community.

He's the founder & co-host of The Product Experience podcast(mindtheproduct.com/podcast) and founder/host of Product in the {A}ether, a virtual lean coffee meetup (pita.social).

Find out more at outofowls.com

Printed in Great Britain
by Amazon